Words of The Nature

Memories Revealed

SACHIN SUMAN

<u>ABOUT</u>

"Words of the Nature: Memories Revealed" is a captivating collection of 14 thought-provoking poems that delve into the realm of nature, offering a unique perspective on its profound connection with memories. Through eloquent language, vivid imagery, and heartfelt expressions, each poem explores different scenes of nature and uncovers the memories they hold.

From the mountain streams to the droplets of rain, and from the enchanting forests to the passing clouds, the poems paint a tapestry of diverse landscapes, each with its own stories to tell. Nature becomes a living entity, speaking through the verses, recounting the memories it has witnessed and absorbed over time.

The collection opens with "Echoes of the Seafoam" a captivating poem that echoes the timeless beauty and allure of the sea. Through vivid imagery and lyrical language, the poem transports readers to the shoreline, where they can feel the gentle caress of the seafoam and hear its whispers carried by the waves. It evokes a sense of wonder and invites contemplation of the ever-changing nature of the ocean.

As the journey continues, we encounter "The Journey of a Brook" where author described the path of the brook and how it makes path from those areas which is still undiscovered by humans.

The poem reflects on the brook's ability to make

ways and memories, symbolizing the continuous

cycle of life.

In "The Enchantment of the Enchanted Forest," a

poem that transports readers into a serene forest

setting. The trees stand tall and proud, their ancient

whispers revealing the secrets they have

safeguarded for generations. The poem invites us to

listen attentively, allowing the memories embedded

within the trees to unfold before our very eyes..

The collection also takes us to the the land of winter

in "The Gentle Breeze of Biting Cold" where the

gentle blow of breeze in winter make us shiver and moan. The poem invites readers to embrace the beauty of land where snow glitters like crystals and appreciate the moments that leave lasting imprints on our souls.

Each poem in "Words of the Nature: Memories Revealed" uncovers a distinct facet of the natural world and the memories it carries. Through the lyrical verses, readers are encouraged to reflect on their own encounters with nature, recognizing the profound impact it has on our lives.

Beyond the picturesque landscapes and scenic vistas, the poems explore the intricate relationship between nature and memories. They remind us that nature is not merely a backdrop to our lives but an active participant, silently recording and preserving the memories that unfold within its embrace.

The collection delves into themes of reflection, nostalgia, and the passage of time. The poems invite readers to connect with their own memories, drawing parallels between personal experiences and the shared memories held by nature. In this introspective journey, readers are encouraged to find solace, inspiration, and a sense of belonging within the intricate tapestry of existence.

The power of "Words of the Nature: Memories Revealed" lies in its ability to evoke emotions and evoke a sense of wonder about the world around us.

Through the carefully crafted poems, the author invites readers to pause, reflect, and appreciate the beauty and significance of nature's memories.

Ultimately, the collection serves as a poignant reminder that nature is not separate from us but an integral part of our own stories. It encourages us to immerse ourselves in the sights, sounds, and sensations of the natural world, allowing its memories to intertwine with our own.

CONTENT

People see loneliness as sadness but for an introvert its uncountable number of unheard poems and imaginary stories.

- SACHIN SUMAN

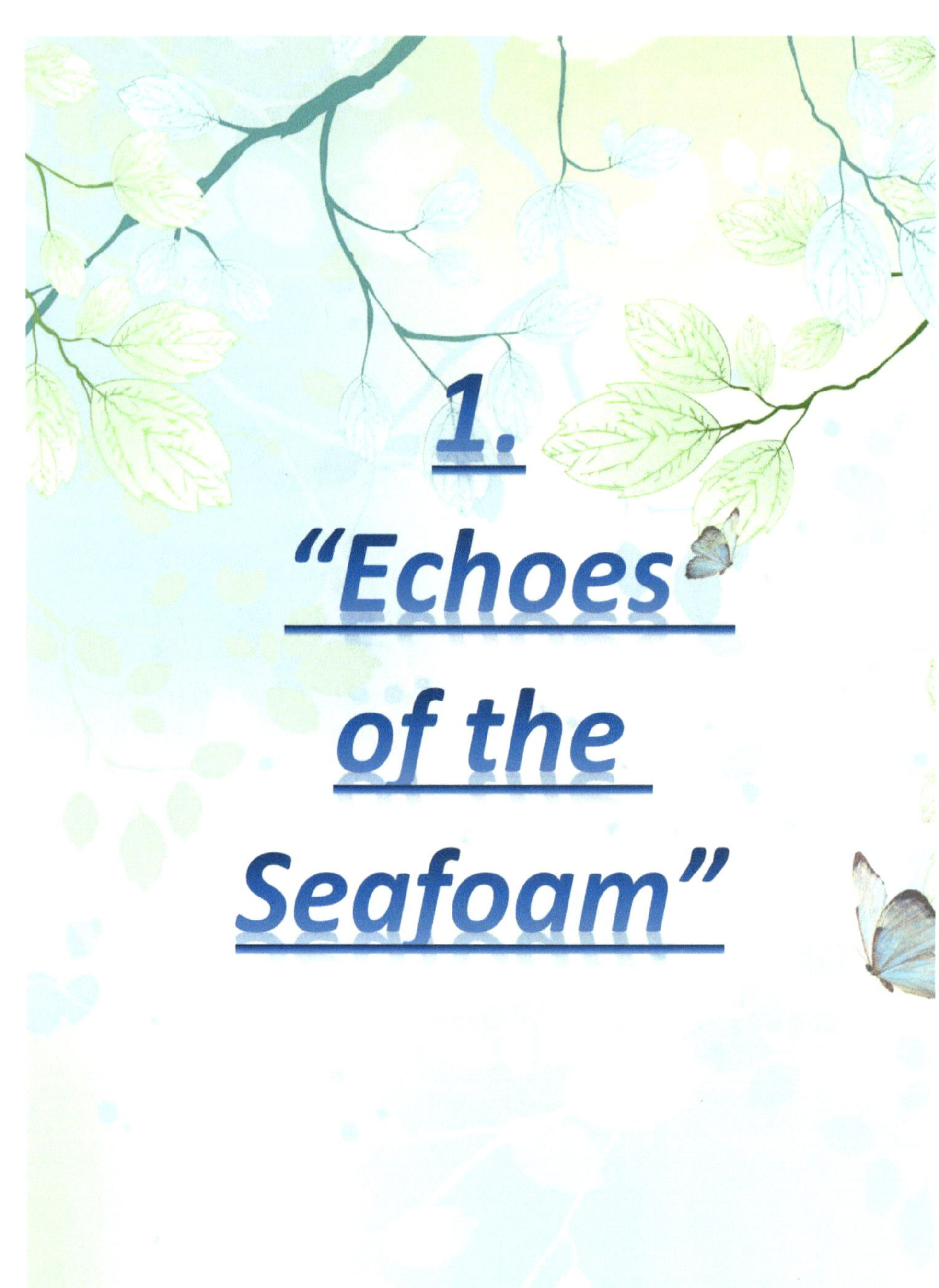

1.
"Echoes
of the
Seafoam"

Echoes of the Seafoam

I hear the echoes of the seafoam,

Whispering secrets from the deep;

The tales of ancient mariners,

And the secrets they did keep.

The foam that dances on the waves,

In rhythm with the tide;

The salty mist that fills the air,

The sea is never shy to hide.

The echoes of the seafoam,

Carried on the breeze;

To distant lands and foreign shores,

Across the seven seas.

I hear the echoes of the seafoam,

In every gentle sound;

The rustling of the sea-grass,

As it sways upon the ground.

The music of the ocean,

Is like a symphony;

The whispers of the seafoam,

Are part of its harmony.

The echoes of the seafoam,

Are like a lullaby;

The gentle ebb and flow of waves,

ill soothe and pacify.

I hear the echoes of the seafoam,

As it calls out to me;

Inviting me to join the dance,

And set my spirit free.

To feel the sand between my toes,

And taste the salty air;

To dive into the ocean blue,

And leave behind all care.

The echoes of the seafoam,

Are like a precious gift;

A memory of the ocean's love,

That forever will uplift.

So when you hear the echoes,

Of the seafoam on the shore;

Remember all its secrets,

And its tales of evermore.

2.

"Whispers of the Willow Tree"

<u>*Whispers of the Willow Tree*</u>

The willow tree stands tall and proud,

Its branches reaching to the sky,

Its leaves a gentle shade of green,

As the wind blows softly by.

And in its boughs, there lies a secret,

Whispers the willow tree,

A tale of love and loss and hope,

A story of eternity.

For in the rustling of its leaves,

A melody begins to play,

A song of wisdom, grace and peace,

That carries on through night and day.

The whispers of the willow tree,

Are like a gentle breeze,

They tell of all the hidden things,

And what the heart believes.

They whisper of a love that's lost,

And the tears that often fall,

Of dreams that never come to be,

And the loneliness of it all.

But in the whispers of the willow tree,

There's also hope and light,

A promise of a brighter day,

And strength to carry on the fight.

Though the willow tree may weep,

Its tears are like a balm,

A healing for the wounded heart,

And a soothing for the soul.

So let the whispers of the willow tree,

Be like a soothing balm,

To mend your heart and lift your spirit,

And bring you peace and calm.

For in its rustling, gentle leaves,

The willow tree will tell,

The secrets of a life well-lived,

And a love that's never failed.

3.

"The Melancholy of the Misty Morning"

The Melancholy of the Misty Morning

The misty morning brings with it,

A melancholy hue,

A somberness that settles in,

And lingers like a dew.

The world is wrapped in mystery,

A shroud that hides the light,

And though the day is dawning,

It feels like endless night.

The silence is a symphony,

A song without a sound,

The stillness of the morning mist,

A world without a bound.

The trees that stand like sentinels,

Are shrouded in the fog,

A world that's lost in memory,

A dream covered with smog.

The melancholy of the misty morning,

Is like a tender kiss,

A whisper of a world beyond,

A promise of pure bliss.

Though the mist may hide the light,

It cannot quench the flame,

That burns within the human heart,

And sets the soul aflame.

And so the misty morning brings,

A melancholy hue,

A bittersweet reminder,

Of all that we've been through.

The memories that we hold,

The ones we've left behind,

The joys and sorrows of our lives,

Are hidden in the misty mind.

But still we rise and face the day,

And walk into the light,

Though the morning may be misty,

The day will still be bright.

And in the misty morning,

We find a sense of peace,

A moment to reflect and breathe,

And let our worries cease.

The melancholy of the misty morning,

Is like a gentle rain,

It washes clean our troubled minds,

And soothes our weary pain.

And though the mist may hide the world,

And make it seem so small,

The morning mist will lift its veil,

And show us life in all.

The melancholy of the misty morning,

Is like a whispered prayer,

A moment to embrace the now,

And leave behind the past we adhere.

For in the misty morning,

We find a beauty rare,

A world beyond the fog and mist,

And life that's everywhere.

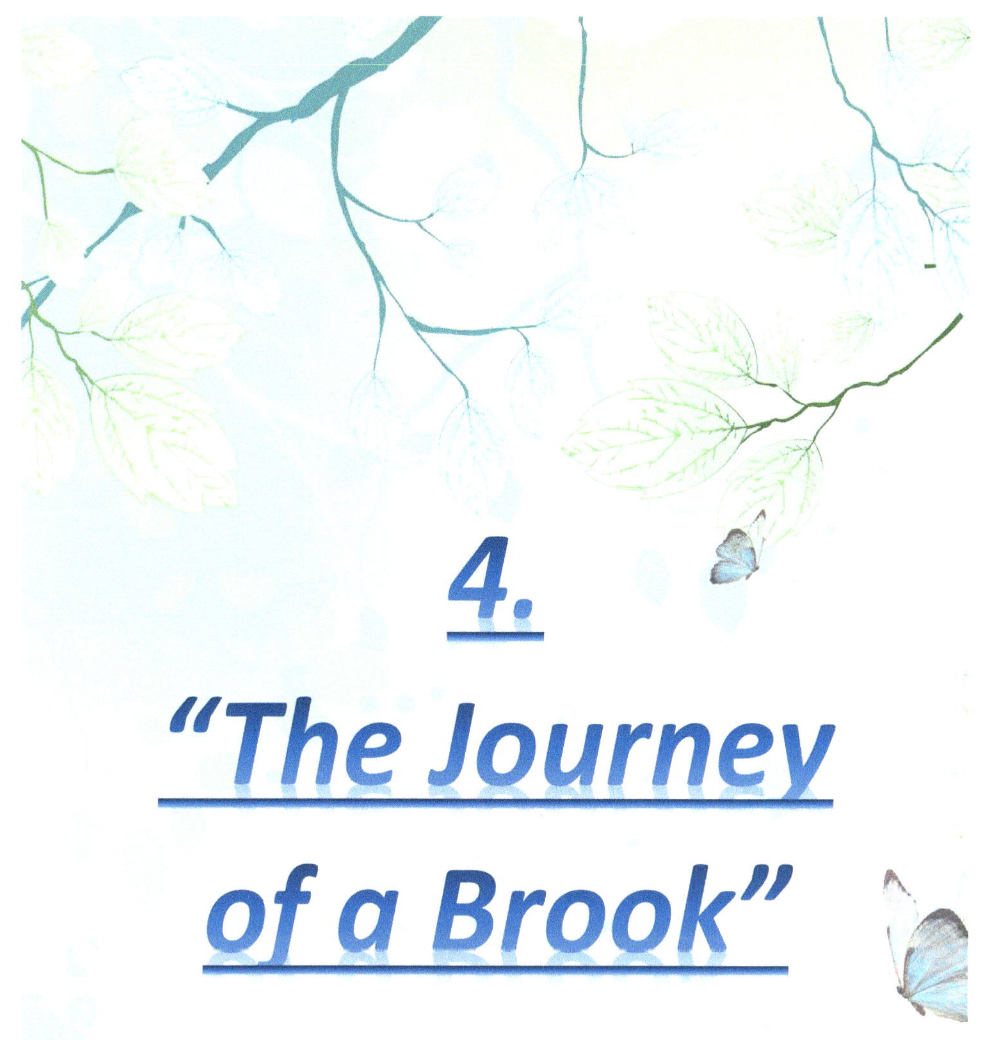

4.

"The Journey of a Brook"

The Journey of a Brook

A path untravelled,

A mystery unsolved;

The journey of a brook,

Life evolved.

Starts from heaven,

Down to Earth;

Somewhere on mountains,

Took its birth.

In the night of moonlight,

At dawn of day;

Shines like a pearl,

White and grey.

It goes and goes,

Passing villages;

From the place it rose,

Down the bridges.

A gift of god,

To humans I say;

A beauty of nature,

Beginning of a day.

5.

"The Secrets of the Starry Nights"

The Secrets of the Starry Night

The night sky is a canvas so vast,

A masterpiece painted with stars that last,

Each one a secret, a mystery untold,

A tale to be uncovered, a story to behold.

The secrets of the starry night,

Are whispered in the moon's soft light,

Of tales of love, joy, and strife,

Of journeys taken throughout life.

The stars above, so bright and bold,

Are secrets that the heavens hold,

Of far-off lands and distant dreams,

Of places unseen and yet to be seen.

The secrets of the starry night,

Are stories of hope, fear, and contrite,

Of path that's lost, and path that's found,

An unending journey of people abound.

The constellations that we see,

Are stories from antiquity,

Of heroes and God, and legends of old,

Their secrets shine bright, so bold.

The shining stars, like light for every site,

Is a pathway to the secrets of the night,

Of mysteries that we have yet to explore,

Of wonders that we have yet to adore.

The secrets of the starry night,

Are whispered in the winds so light,

Of a universe so vast, so grand,

Of a world beyond what we understand. 

So let us gaze upon the stars,

And listen to the whispers from afar,

For in their secrets, we can find,

The beauty of life, so wild, so kind. 

The secrets of the starry night,

Are stories that we can bring to light,

Of love, of hope, and joy,

Of journeys taken throughout life.

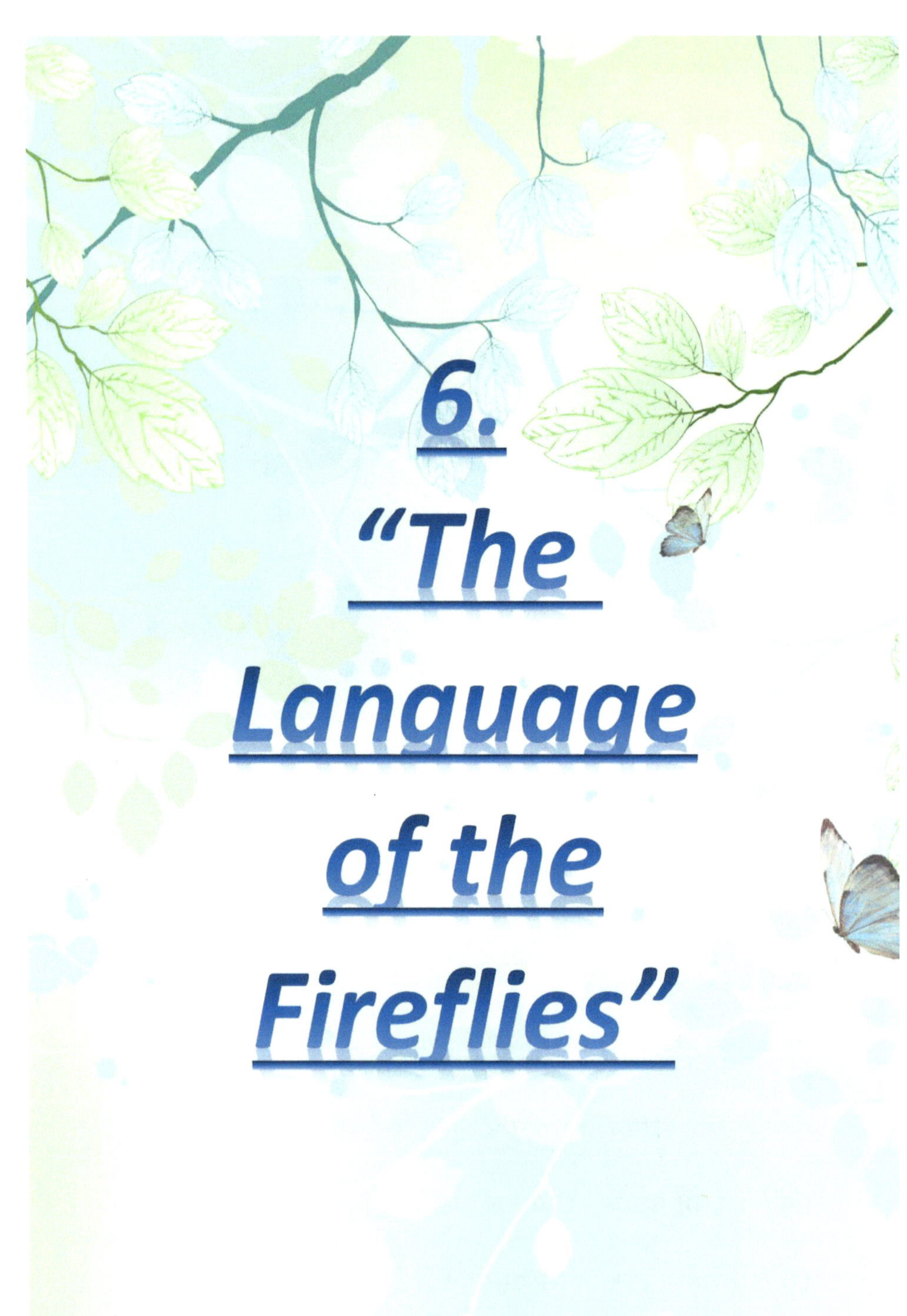

6. "The Language of the Fireflies"

<u>*The Language of the Fireflies*</u>

In the summer's warm embrace,

The fireflies come to play;

Dancing through the evening sky,

With light that shows the way.

They twinkle and they shimmer,

Like stars that touch the ground;

And in their gentle language,

A wondrous world is found.

The language of the fireflies,

Is like a secret code;

A message to the universe,

Of love, hope and growth.

For in their flickering movements,

A story can be told;

Of life and all its mysteries,

That often go untold.

They speak of magic in the night,

Of wonder in the day;

They show us that the world is vast,

And has much more to say.

The language of the fireflies,

Is like a gentle hum;

A symphony full of melody tunes,

that makes the spirit numb.

From their glowing bodies,

A truth can be revealed;

the light of hope we forget to see,

And all the things we feel.

They speak of joy and happiness,

Of love, peace and light;

They show us that the world is good,

And worth living with might.

The language of the fireflies,

Is like a gentle breeze;

That carries with it all the hopes,

Of all that we may please.

For in their gentle movements,

A truth can be unveiled;

The things of past we never let go,

And all the peace to find we failed.

They speak of growth and learning,

Of taking on the world;

They show us that the path is hard,

But it worth in the end.

The language of the fireflies,

Is like a gentle hand;

That guides us through the darkness,

And helps us understand.

In their flickering light,

A truth can be embraced;

Of all the stuffs we are meant to be,

And all the things we face.

So let the language of the fireflies,

Guide us through the night;

And fill our mind with peace and delight,

And all that is just right.

From their glowing bodies,

A story can be told;

Of life and all its mysteries,

That often go untold.

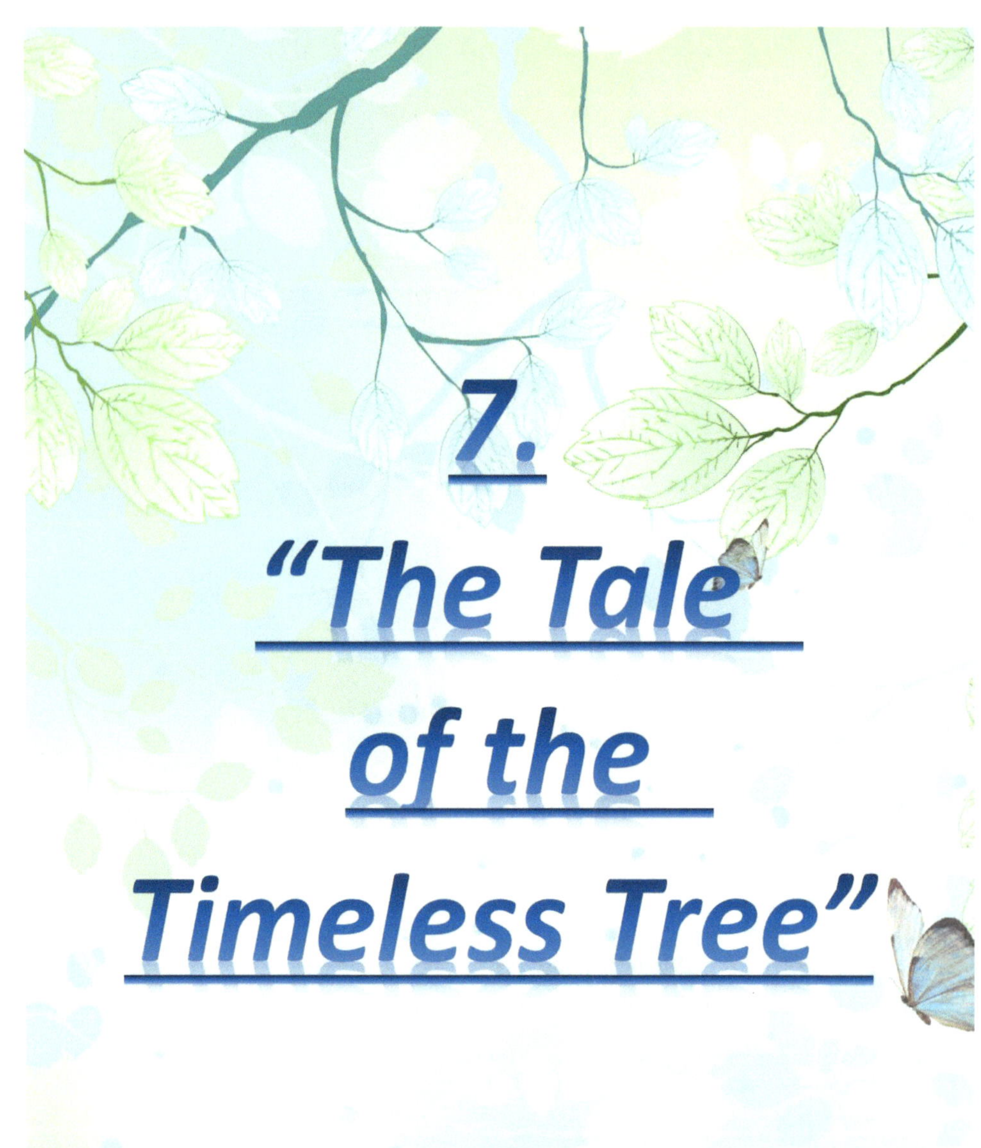

7.

"The Tale of the Timeless Tree"

The Tale of the Timeless Tree

In a deep forest with vast land,

Stood a tree so old and grand;

Its roots ran deep, its branches wide,

A guardian of the wild inside.

The tale of this timeless tree,

Was one of beauty, strength, and mystery;

For centuries it had stood,

Through droughts and floods, through storms and good.

Its bark was rough, its leaves were green,

A symbol of life that could be seen;

And through the years it watched and waited,

As the world around it shifted and fated.

Many creatures came to dwell,

Within the shade this tree did spell;

Birds and squirrels, rabbits and deer,

All found their home within its sphere.

But there was more to this tree than what met the

eye,

For it held a secret, hidden deep inside;

A force so strong, so pure and true,

That time itself, it could see through.

For as the years went by and by,

This tree remained steadfast, never to die;

It saw the rise and fall of men,

And the endless cycle that goes again and again.

It knew the secrets of the land,

And held the wisdom of the grand;

For in its roots and in its leaves,

Were secrets that could set us free.

And though the world around it changed,

This tree remained, unaltered and unchanged;

A constant reminder of what could be,

If we too learned to live so free.

For in this timeless tree we see,

An image of all those we can be;

A force so strong, so pure and true,

That time itself, it could see through.

So let us honor this ancient tree,

And all the wonder that it brings us free;

For in its tale we find our own,

And all the seeds of life that have been sown.

8.
"The Memories of the Mountain Stream"

The Memories of the Mountain Stream

In the mountains large and high,

There flows a stream, so pure like sky;

Its water clear as crystal gleams,

As it sparkles in the sun's bright beams.

The memories of this mountain stream,

Are ones of joy, hope, and dream;

In its flowing water flows,

The tales of life, the highs and lows.

It starts its journey up on high,

A source of life that will never die;

Its journey is long, its path so clear,

It flows on and on without any fear.

It twists and turns, it bends like winds,

As it weaves its way through the rocks and binds;

And as it flows, it carries on,

The secrets of the world, both new and gone.

In its water, we can see,

The flow of memories, joy, sorrow and flee;

The ancient rocks, the fallen trees,

The stories of the land and its mysteries.

The mountain stream is like a book,

Of all the things we've come to look;

A story of the world and all its ways,

The secrets of the land that it displays.

And as we walk along its shore,

We feel the magic that it pours;

A tale of wonder, hope, and might,

A journey that can set things right.

In its flowing water, we can see,

The beauty of life, a journey carefree;

The laughter and tears, the joy and pain,

The memories that will forever remain.

And as we pause to listen in,

To the sound of water's gentle spin,

We hear a voice, so clear and true,

A whisper of life, that's always new.

The mountain stream is like a friend,

On whom we can always depend;

An origin of life, a ray of light,

A journey that can make things right.

And as we walk along its bank,

We feel the magic, the hope, and the thanks;

For all that it gives, and all that it knows,

The memories of life that forever flows.

The memories of the mountain stream,

Are ones that fill our hearts with gleam;

For in its flowing water lies,

The secrets of the world, the lows and highs.

So in this moment let's take a pause,

And feel the wonder of nature and applause;

For in the pristine water, we see,

The beauty of nature, the memories of mountain stream.

9.

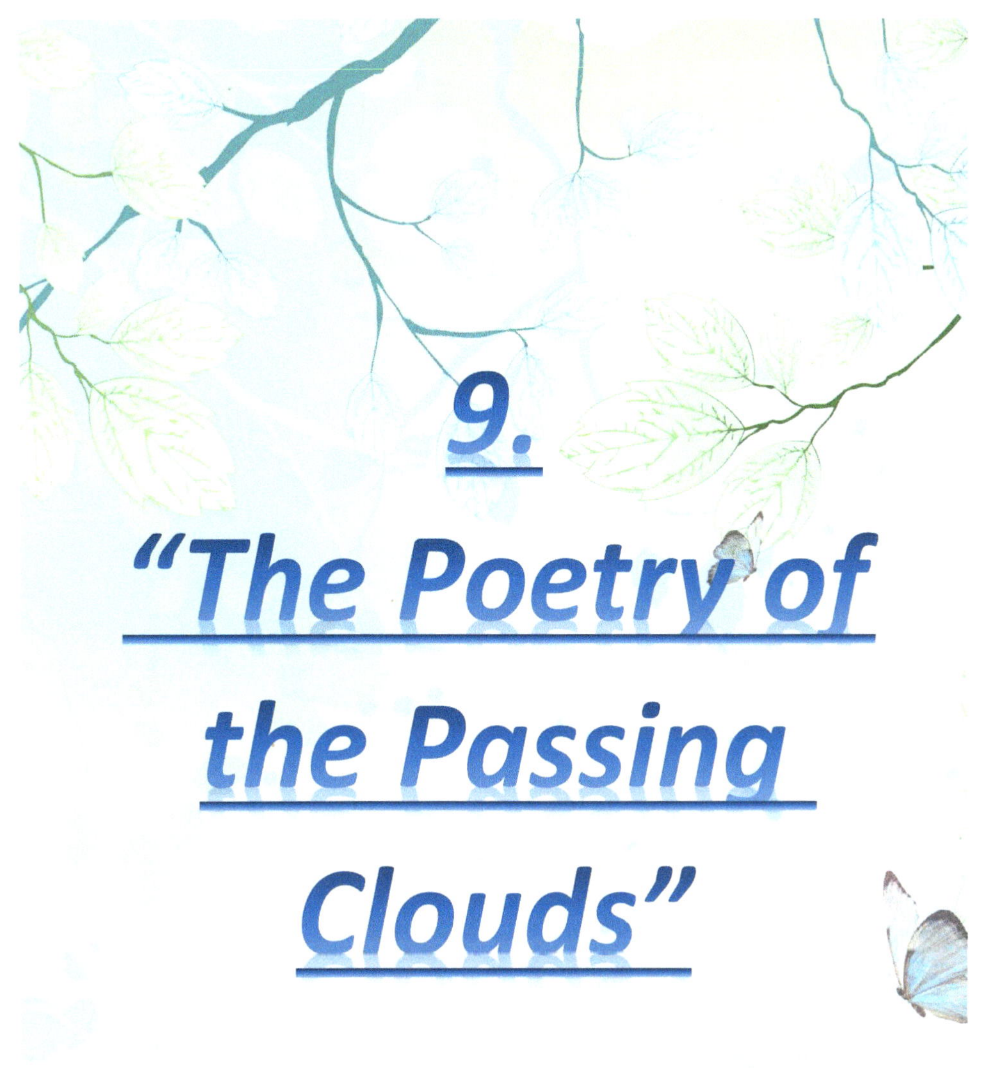

"The Poetry of the Passing Clouds"

<u>The Poetry of the Passing Clouds</u>

The passing clouds, like poetry,

Drift across the sky so free;

A canvas for the sun to paint,

A tapestry of hues so quaint.

They dance and swirl, they glide and flow,

In patterns that we'll never know;

And as they pass, they leave behind,

A trail of magic, one of a kind.

For in their beauty, we can see,

A poetry of life, so free;

A song of freedom, hope, and light,

That fills the sky with all its might.

The clouds, they speak a language rare,

A poetry of life that we can share;

They tell the tales of nature's art,

A symphony that fills our heart.

The shapes they form, the hues they bring,

A canvas for the soul to sing;

A melody of life and light,

Shines bright, both day and night.

For in their dance, we can find,

A world of wonder, peace in mind;

A poetry of life like sky so grand,

That fills our hearts and makes us stand.

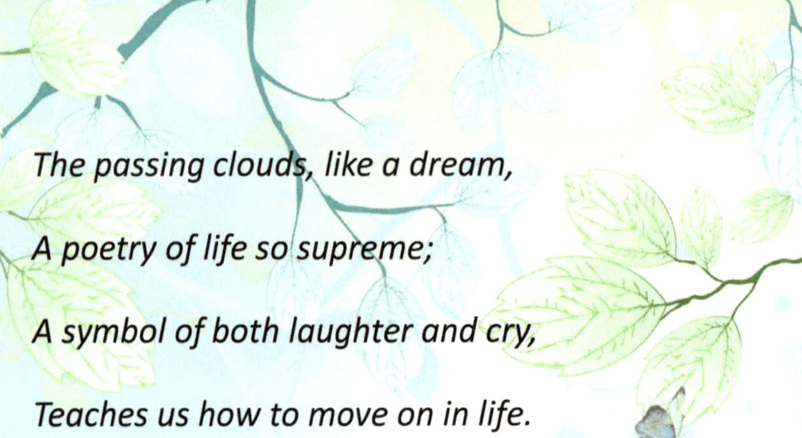

The passing clouds, like a dream,

A poetry of life so supreme;

A symbol of both laughter and cry,

Teaches us how to move on in life.

The passing clouds are like a song,

A melody sweet, so clear, so strong;

A symphony of life, so wild and free,

A journey of hope, for all to see.

10.

"The
Enchantment
of the
Enchanted
Forest"

The Enchantment of the Enchanted Forest

In the heart of the woods, so lush and green,

Lies a place so enchanting, a world unseen,

A place where the trees speak in whispers low,

And the secrets of nature, so wild, so slow.

Here, in the enchanted forest, the air is alive,

With the rustling of leaves, and the buzzing of hive,

And the gentle breeze, like a whispering friend,

Carries the stories, that nature intends.

The place, where the sunlight filters through,

And the sound of the river, is like a song so true,

Nature speaks, in a language so pure,

That the mind of the world is so easy to cure.

Here, in the enchanted forest, the trees stand tall,

Like ancient guardians, so proud, so bold,

And the rustling of leaves, like a gentle call,

Is a reminder, of the stories they hold.

The forest speaks in a language so clear,

Of the beauty of life, of the love that we fear,

Of the joy of laughter, and the pain of tears,

Of the endless journey, throughout the years.

And as we walk, through the enchanted wood,

We feel the magic, the wonder and the good,

Of all that is, and all that can be,

The beauty of life, so peaceful, so free.

In the enchanted forest, the world comes alive,

And the magic of nature, like a beacon, does thrive,

And the whispers of the trees, and the rustling of leaves,

Is a reminder, of the beauty, that nature believes.

So let us take a moment, to feel the embrace,

Of the enchanted forest, and its magical grace,

And listen to the stories, that nature does share,

The beauty of life, and the love that we bear.

In the place, where the world is so still,

We can hear the whispers, that nature instills,

The magic of life, the wonder of earth,

And the joy of love, that gives life its worth.

So let us embrace, the enchantment of the forest,

And let nature speak, in a language so honest,

In its whispers, we can find the key,

the beauty of life, so peaceful, so free.

11.

"The Droplets of Rain"

<u>The Droplets of Rain</u>

The droplets of rain, fall so hard,

On the outskirts of the city, in the yard,

A symphony of sound, a music so pure,

As the raindrops falls, it treats as a cure.

The wind howls, and the trees sway,

As the droplets of rain, come down to play,

The scent of earth, so lively and fresh,

Fills the air, with a fragrance afresh.

The raindrops hit the ground with force,

As the storm rages on, without remorse,

The lightning flashes, the thunder roars,

As the droplets of rain, open new doors.

The droplets of rain, cleanse the earth,

Washing away the dust and the dirt,

Replenishing the land, with water so pure,

A precious gift, of that we can be sure.

The droplets of rain, speak to me,

Of nature's power, of its majesty,

Of life and death, of birth and renewal,

A cycle of nature, so eternal.

So let the droplets of rain, fall where they want,

On the roof or terrace, or   the plant,

They bring with them, a gift so true,

Of life, growth, and hope anew.

12.

"Echoes of Bliss: Nature's Calming Voice"

<u>**_"Echoes of Bliss: Nature's Calming Voice"_**</u>

In nature's realm, where tranquility thrives,

Echoes of bliss in every breeze that arrives,

Whispers of solace carried on gentle wings,

Nature's calming voice, the melody it sings.

A symphony of birds greets the dawn,

Their harmonies, a soothing balm to spawn,

Their melodies, like ripples on a serene lake,

Guiding hearts and minds for tranquility's sake.

The rustling leaves dance in the golden light,

A gentle sway, a mesmerizing sight,

Their whispers echo tales of ancient trees,

Of timeless wisdom and nature's mysteries.

The babbling brook, its murmur soft and low,

Flows with grace, its rhythm in tranquil flow,

Its gentle currents, a lullaby to the soul,

As nature's calming voice seeks to console.

The fragrance of flowers, a fragrant embrace,

Aromas that beckon, a sensory trace,

Lavender and jasmine on the gentle breeze,

Aromatherapy, nature's gift to ease.

The rustling grasses, a gentle lullaby,

Their hushed tones sing of a tranquil sky,

Caressed by the wind, their whispers rise,

Nature's calming voice, a solace in disguise.

The sun sets, casting hues of orange and gold,

A tapestry of colours, stories untold,

The sky was ablaze with celestial art,

Nature's masterpiece, a soothing balm to impart.

Beneath the starry canopy, a celestial veil,

Twinkling lights, a calming celestial trail,

Each constellation, a map of peace,

Guiding weary souls to serenity's release.

The moon, a radiant presence in the night,

Casting its glow, a comforting light,

Its tranquil beams, a serene touch,

Nature's calming voice, soothing music by bruch .

The waves upon the shore, a rhythmic song,

Soothing melodies that carry along,

Their ebb and flow, a dance of pure delight,

Nature's calming voice, embracing the night.

The mountain peaks, majestically tall,

Reach for the heavens, standing proud and all,

Their silent strength, an embodiment of peace,

Nature's calming voice, a refuge to release.

Through meadows and forests, nature's serene domain,

A sanctuary where calm and peace reign,

In every breath, its gentle touch we feel,

Nature's calming voice, a love that's real.

So let us heed the echoes of bliss,

Nature's calming voice, a timeless kiss,

In its embrace, find solace and rest,

A sanctuary where our souls are blessed.

For nature's calming voice, it knows,

The secrets to soothe, to heal, to compose,

In its harmonies, we find our repose,

Echoes of bliss, where serenity flows.

In nature's realm, let peace abide,

Embraced by echoes of bliss, side by side,

Nature's calming voice, a melody forever,

Will guide us to tranquility now and ever.

13.

"The Gentle Breeze of Biting Cold"

"The Gentle Breeze of Biting Cold"

In a land of winter, I was told,

Where the gentle breeze blows in the biting cold,

I'll tell a tale in a simple, childish tone,

Of the chilly winds that make you shiver and moan.

Oh, the gentle breeze of biting cold,

It sweeps through the land so fiercely and bold,

But fear not, my friends, coz I'll unfold,

A story of warmth that will make your hearts to

hold.

When the frosty winds begin to blow,

And the snowflakes dance, falling in a row,

Wrap up tight in coats and scarves so bold,

And step outside, let the adventure unfold.

The gentle breeze whispers secrets in your ear,

Of snow-covered hills, oh so crystal clear,

It tickles your cheeks and makes you feel alive,

As you explore the wintry world, oh, how you

thrive!

With rosy cheeks and noses bright pink,

You build snowmen and have a snowball fight,

With laughter and joy, your spirits take flight,

In the midst of winter's chill, everything feels right.

The biting cold may nip at your toes,

But with each breath, your excitement grows,

In this frosty wonderland, you look,

A world full of magic, like a fairy-tale book.

The gentle breeze carries stories untold,

Of frozen lakes where ice skaters glide so bold,

With graceful moves, they twirl and spin,

Creating art on ice is a beautiful win.

You join them too, with cautious delight,

Sliding and gliding, under the pale moonlight,

The crisp air fills the lungs, oh, what a sight,

The gentle breeze whispers, "This is pure delight!"

As the day draws to an end, and the sun goes down,

The stars twinkle brightly, wearing a frosty crown,

The gentle breeze softly sings a lullaby,

As you cuddle up, under a starry sky.

You dream of winter adventures, far and wide,

Of sledging down hills, with glee and pride,

Of sipping hot cocoa by the cozy fire,

As the gentle breeze of biting cold inspires.

So, my dear friends, embrace the winter's chill,

Let the gentle breeze of biting cold give you a thrill,

For within its icy touch, you'll find,

A world of wonder, that warms the heart and mind.

The gentle breeze of biting cold it holds,

Magic that only winter unfolds,

So bundle up, and let your spirit take flight,

As you embrace the cold with all your might.

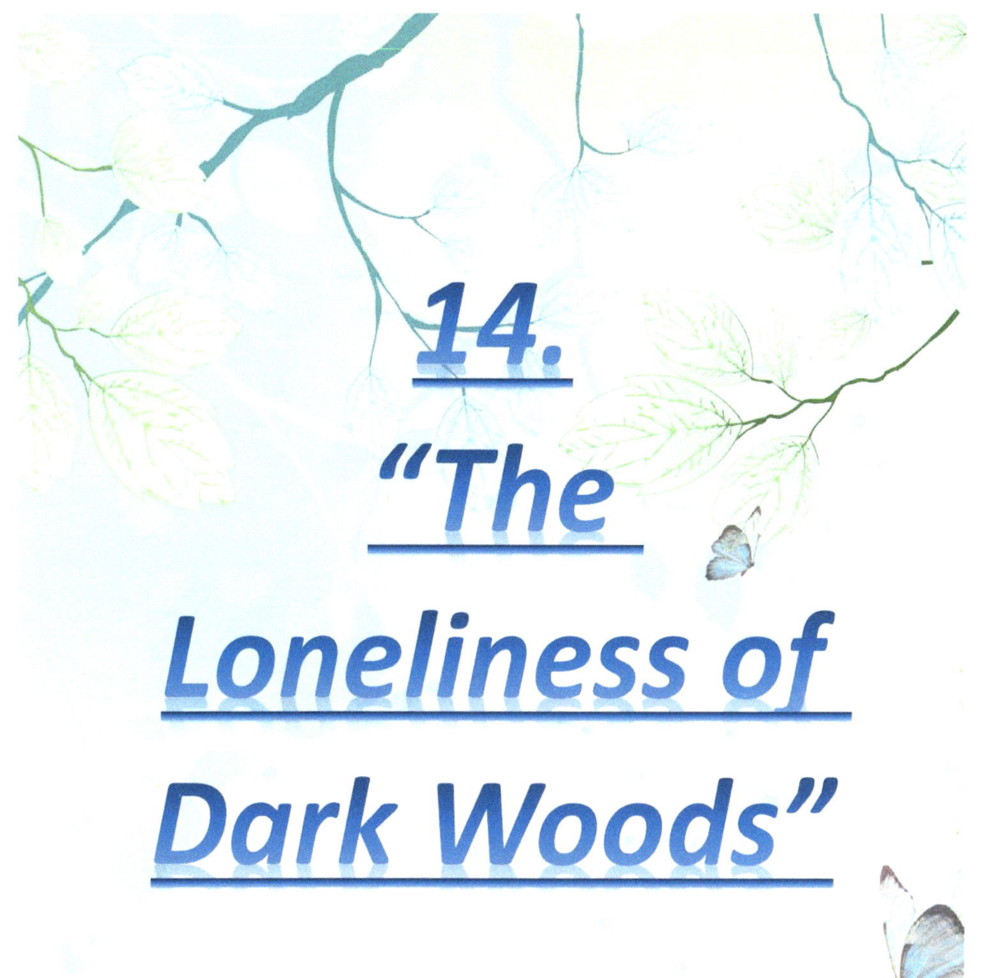

14.
"The
Loneliness of
Dark Woods"

<u>***The Loneliness of Dark Woods***</u>

In the hush of twilight, when the sun descends,

The woods awaken as the daylight ends;

A veil of shadows cloaks the towering trees,

And a whispered solitude floats on the breeze.

The darkness creeps in like a secret unfurled,

As the night claims its kingdom, in the ancient world;

The forest stands silent, its secrets concealed,

And the loneliness of dark woods is revealed.

The leaves rustle softly, a gentle lullaby,

As the creatures of the night begin to pry,

The owl hoots mournfully, a haunting cry,

Piercing the stillness, reaching the sky.

The moon emerges, casting a silver glow,

Illuminating the path where shadows grow,

Its ethereal light, like a beacon of hope,

Guiding lost souls through the darkness, they cope.

Beneath the canopy, branches entwined,

The quiet of the woods speaks to the mind;

An echo of footsteps, so timid and light,

Whispers of loneliness in the heart of the night.

The gentle rustle of nocturnal creatures,

Navigating the maze of nature's features,

Their eyes gleaming with a mysterious sheen,

In the depths of darkness, their presence unseen.

The scent of damp earth lingers in the air,

As the night reveals its secrets with care,

The fragrance of moss and decaying wood,

A reminder of nature's cycle understood.

As I wander deeper into the heart of the woods,

A sense of isolation, a feeling that intrudes,

The rustling leaves, like distant sighs,

Evoke a sense of longing, that never dies.

The wind whispers secrets in the thick of the trees,

Carrying tales of forgotten melodies,

Of forgotten lives that once roamed this land,

Their echoes resonating, hand in hand.

The loneliness of dark woods, it speaks,

Through the silence that dwells, so quiet, so bleak,

It draws you in, like an invisible force,

Into the depths where solitude takes its course.

But in this loneliness, beauty is found,

A profound connection, deep underground,

In the quietude, the soul finds repose,

In the embrace of darkness, where true solace grows.

The night sky above, adorned with stars,

Each one has a story, shimmering from afar,

They twinkle with brilliance, a celestial dance,

Mirroring the beauty of the dark woods' expanse.

The moonlight filters through the tangled trees,

Casting enchanting patterns upon the leaves,

A gentle illumination, soft and serene,

Revealing the hidden, the mystical unseen.

In the loneliness of dark woods, a symphony plays,

Of rustling leaves and nocturnal displays,

Of distant howls and whispered songs,

A tapestry of nature's serenades for long.

So, let me wander, in the solitude of the night,

Embracing the darkness, without a hint of fright,

For within this loneliness, a connection is found,

A harmony between nature and the soul, profound.

In the depths of the woods, where shadows reside,

The loneliness whispers, a companion by my side,

And as I lose myself in its embrace,

I find solace and discover my inner grace.